Author:

Jephita Oeke Otuke

Published by:

CreateSpace

ISBN-13: 978-1514280546
ISBN-10: 151428054X

Table of Contents

Acknowledgement

I would like to thank my wife Beatrice for standing beside me throughout the period of writing this book. She always made sure that I had a cap of coffee while I was on my computer working on this book. In a special way I also thank my wonderful children Brian, Cynthia and Kelvin for whom I dedicate this book to. I would not stop thanking my friend and great author Julius Wambwa for encouraging me to start writing.

About This Book

This book has been written from research on the best teaching practices and a variety of creative ideas. The salient features of this book are:

- ➢ Establishing clarity of thought and developing computer fluency is the main objective of Computer Whiz Book One.
- ➢ Fun is an important element of learning.
- ➢ The lesson contents are woven around interactions between an imaginary teacher and two students.
- ➢ The teacher mostly asks questions that guide the students to discover and learn topics on their own.
- ➢ Each lesson focuses on specific concepts and associated skills. These concepts are selected such that:
  - o They lay a strong foundation for learning computers.
  - o They contribute towards general intellectual development
  - o They are age appropriate.
- ➢ The Worksheets and Activities are designed in such a way that they supplement topics being covered in other subjects, to the extent possible. Group activities are included in each lesson to encourage collaborative learning. Projects are also suggested to reinforce the learning of topics across multiple lessons.
- ➢ 21st century skills of critical thinking, collaboration, communication and creativity are addressed in the lesson content and supplementary activities.
- ➢ The book meets the standards suggested for continuous and comprehensive evaluation (Right to education).
- ➢ The book includes child friendly illustrations that are sensitive to body and image.
- ➢ Comments on the book and suggestions may be sent to (greatgsc@gmail.com).

How to Use This Book

This book is meant to be used for teaching computers to children in a way that is mostly fun. The teacher's role is primarily that of a facilitator encouraging active learning. Specific guidelines for each lesson can be found in the Teacher's Guide for each lesson available separately. Ensure that the conceptual understanding is mastered before proceeding to the skills. In the computer lab, if they are doing activities in groups, ensure that they switch "drivers" frequently, so that each student gets to do a fair amount of the computer based activities.

The Worksheets include exercises to inculcate higher order thinking skills. Use the Group Activities and Projects to stimulate creativity and knowledge sharing. The book is designed so that it can be covered comfortably in one year, with one class (30 to 45 minutes) per week. See the table below for an overview of the concepts, skills and values covered in each lesson along with a week wise schedule.

Lesson No.	Topic Name	Concepts	Skills	Values reinforced	Weeks
1	Uuse of Computers	• What are uses of a computer	• Identify places where computers are used	• Developing good habits • Awareness • Communication	1st – 4th
2	Parts of a Computer	• Computer has many parts	• Know the parts and their functions	• Awareness	5th – 7th
3	Do's and Don'ts with Computers	• Correct way of using computers	• Cleanness • Safety • Carefulness	• Taking precautions • Sensitive to others needs • Sharing resources • Maintaining cleanness	8th – 10th
4	How to use a Mouse	• Functions of a Mouse	• Controlling the pointer and using the left, right clicks and double click	• Following instructions • Understanding what to do	11th – 12th
REVISION					**13th – 14th**
5	How to use a Keyboard	• Functions of a Keyboard	• Entering words and numbers	• Observation of skills	15th – 18th
6, 7	How to Paint using a computer	• Icons, Tools and Toolbar (through example of painting application)	• Open draw and save paint files • Save and print paint files • Quitting the paint activity	• Relating new knowledge to previous learning • Curiosity – observing • Thinking – questioning	19th – 23rd
8	How to Play Music on a Computer	• One of the many things you can do with a Computer	• Open the Media Player • Open a Music File • Use of control buttons, play, pause stop etc.	• Being sensitive to others needs	24th – 25th
9	Knowing your Desktop	• Elements of Windows on a Desktop	• Opening activities on a desktop • To Maximise, Minimise and closing windows	• Neatness	26th – 28th
10	Projects				29th – 32nd

Lesson **1**

Uses of Computers

 In this lesson you will learn a few simple and interesting uses of a computer.

Teacher: Hello! What shall we learn today? Yes, we'll learn what computers can do. We can play games, listen to music, and watch movies on a computer.

Brian: Can we also draw pictures?

Teacher: Sure, you can. A computer can be used for many simple tasks like:

Drawing pictures

Writing letters

Playing games

Listening to music

Adding numbers

Watching movies and cartoons

Cynthia: I remember seeing a computer in our school library.

Brian: I have also seen it, but what is a computer doing in a library?

Teacher: Good question. Let me give some examples of how a computer is used in many places.

1. Airports

Airports use computers to book tickets. They also use them to maintain airplanes timings. When you go with your parents to book tickets, the clerk uses the computer to see if seats are available. Then he takes the money and issues your tickets.

2. Library

A library stores many books. Searching for your favourite book can take a lot of time. So, the library uses a computer to store a list of books and their location. When you want to borrow a book, the librarian can check the computer to see if it is available. Then he can tell you where to find it. He also uses the computer to issue the book to you.

3. Banks

Many people use banks to keep their money safe. The banks use computers to store a list of people and their accounts. When your parents want money to buy something, they go to the bank. The clerk checks on the computer to see if they have enough money in their account. Then the clerk gives the money to your parents.

Cynthia: Ok, but how can children use a computer?

Teacher: Let us see some simple tasks that you can do using a computer.

 You can watch cartoons and movies

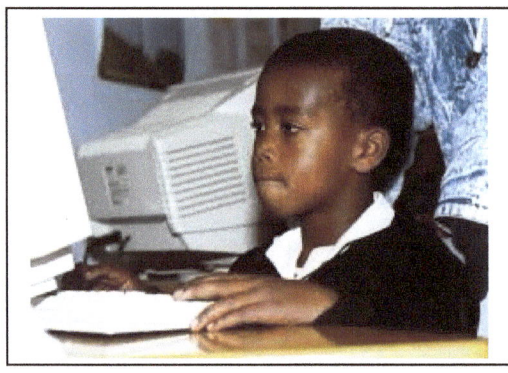 You can draw a picture

 You can listen to music

 You can make greeting cards

Teacher In our daily life we use machines like television, radio, washing machine, mixer, music system, telephone etc. A computer can also do the work of some of these machines.

A Television is used to watch movies.
Can you watch movies on a Computer?

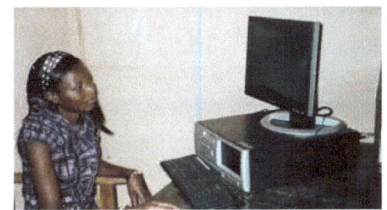

Yes, you can!

The radio system is playing a song.
Can you play a song on a computer?

Yes, you can!

Jane is drawing on a paper.
Yes, he can!

Can she draw using a computer?

Yes, he can!

You can make fresh fruit juice in your mixer.
Can a computer be used like a mixer?
No, it cannot!

You can use a fridge to keep food items.
Can a computer be used like a fridge?
No, it cannot!

You can wash clothes in your wasnıng machine.
Can a computer be used like a washing machine?
No, it cannot!

Brian: Oh, the computer is very clever. Can it do everything?

Teacher: A computer can help you do several things. But there are also many things that it cannot do.

Brian: Why are there so many wires around the computer?

Teacher: We will talk about it when we meet next. Goodbye for now, Bye-Bye...

Learning Outcome

After you have studied this lesson,
you will be able to:
- List the various uses of a computer.
- Identify places where computer can be used.
- Decide when a computer cannot be used.

WORKSHEETS 1

1. Following are some places where computers can be used.
   Match the name with the pictures.

a. Airport   b. Hospital   c. Bank

d. Railway station   e. Library   f. School

e.

2. Here are some places where computers are used. Find them all!

Bank
School
Airport
Hospital
Office
Station
Shop

P	Y	T	R	D	X	K	H	B
S	T	A	T	I	O	N	O	A
H	N	W	S	M	I	H	S	N
S	C	H	O	O	L	N	P	K
O	U	S	G	J	Z	X	I	C
O	F	F	I	C	E	B	T	T
A	X	S	H	O	P	V	A	A
A	I	R	P	O	R	T	L	L

WORKSHEETS 1

3. In what activities can computers be used? Place a tick ✔ mark where you think they can be used and a cross ✘ mark where you think they cannot be used.

a. Janet is eating something. Can a computer be used for eating?

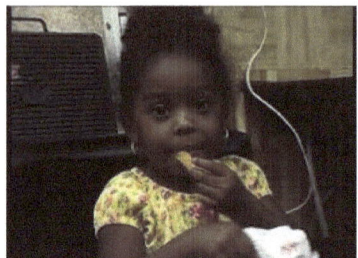

b. Florence is listening to music. Can a computer be used to listen to music?

c. Fred has prepared a list of invitees for his birthday. Can a computer be used for writing the list?

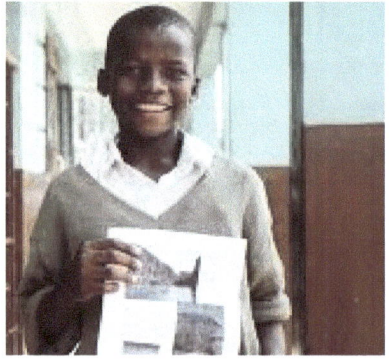

d. Faith is blowing a balloon. Can a computer be used for blowing balloons?

WORKSHEETS 1

a. Francis is adding numbers on a slate. Can he use a computer to add numbers?

b. Collins is drawing. Can a computer be used to draw?

c. Susan is cooking. Can a computer be used to cook?

Activity 1

1. Draw a picture: Request the teacher to open Paint.
    Click Start => All programs => Accessories => Paint

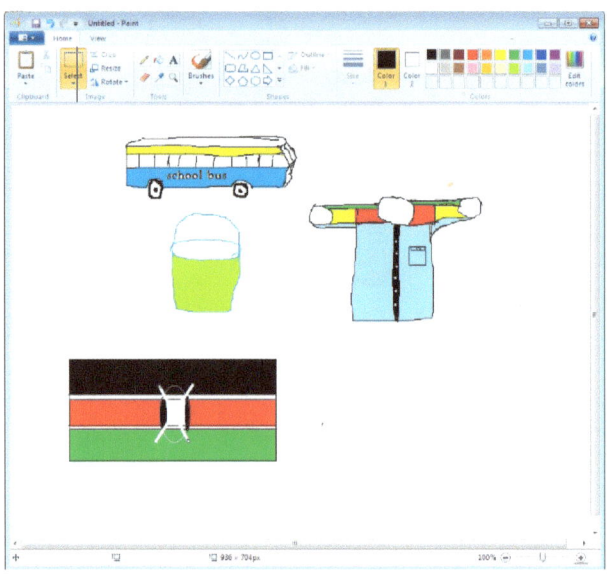

2. Play games: Request the teacher to open them for you.
Click Start => All Programs => Games

Project
Do project 1 given in lesson 10.

Explore!
1. Have you seen any computers in your school?
2. Have you noticed a computer being used at other places?
3. What were they being used for?

Lesson **2**

Parts of a Computer

In this lesson you will learn about the main parts of a computer.

Brian and Cynthia were in the computer room, looking at one of the computers. They were trying to see how the wires were connected together, when the teacher appeared...

Teacher: So, have you already noticed that a computer has many parts?

Brian: Yes, just like we have hands, legs, eyes and ears! What are the names for the parts of a computer?

Teacher: The names of the four most important parts are - **CPU, Monitor, Keyboard,** and **Mouse**.

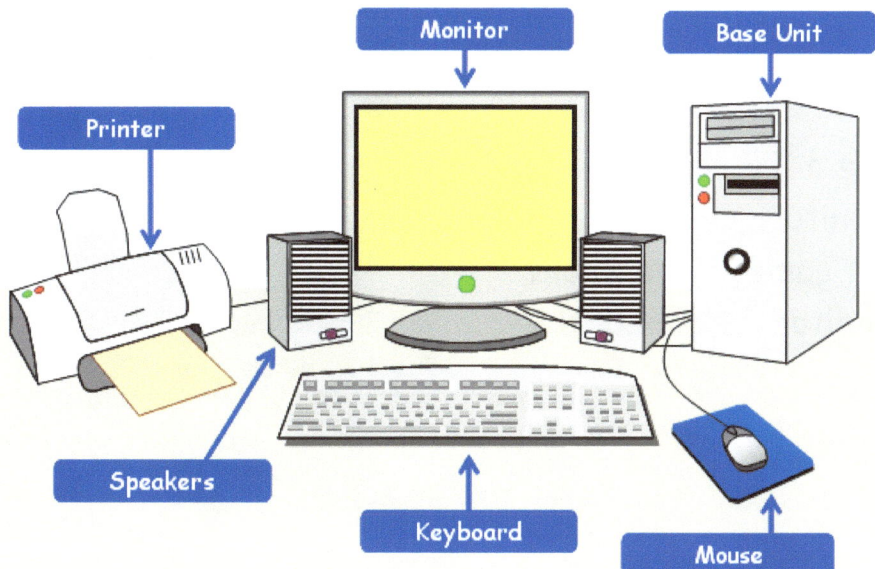

Cythia: Why does a computer need so many parts? What do they do? How are they connected?

Teacher: Good questions! Let us learn about each of these parts.

CPU

CPU (central processing unit) is the most important part of a computer. It is like the brain. It does all the tasks that we want the computer to do. It also controls all the other parts, like the Monitor, Keyboard and Mouse. These parts have to be connected to the CPU, for them to work.

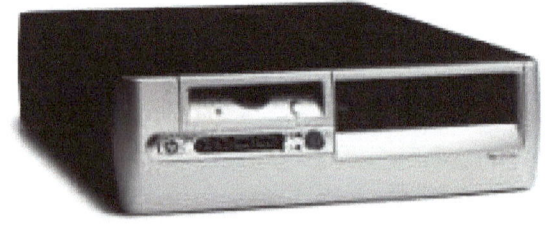

Keyboard

The keyboard is made of several small buttons called **keys**. Each key has a number, letter or word written on it. Just as you use a pencil to write on a paper, you can use a keyboard to write with a computer.

Monitor

A monitor looks like a TV screen. The CPU uses the monitor to show us photos, movies and games. The front portion of the monitor is called the screen, or display.

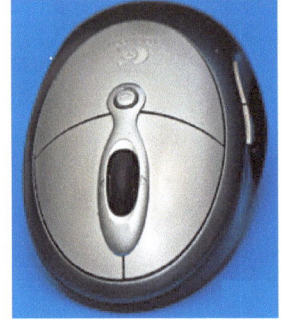

Mouse

A mouse is used to point at items shown on the monitor. The mouse usually has two or three buttons and a small wheel between the buttons.

Brian: You said that we can draw pictures using the computer. Can I use a mouse for drawing? How can I take the picture home?

Teacher: Yes! You can use the mouse to draw pictures. But, you need a **Printer** to print your picture and take it home.

Cythia: You said that we can listen to songs on the computer. From which of these parts do we hear the song?

Teacher: Not from any of these parts. We need **Speakers** to listen to songs. Remember, the speakers, printer or any other part will work only if they are connected to the CPU.

Brian picks up the computer mouse and starts playing with it.

Brian: What are these buttons for?

Teacher: Be careful! We must take proper care of the different computer parts.
Tomorrow we will learn how to do this and then we will learn about the buttons.
Bye-Bye...

Learning Outcome
After you have studied this lesson,
you will be able to:

- Name the main parts of a computer.
- Describe functions of these parts.

WORKSHEETS 2

1. Colour the parts of the computer as follows:
    Monitor in Yellow, CPU in Blue, Keyboard in Green, and mouse in Red.

2. Identify which are the parts of the computer and circle them.

CPU   Key   Rat   PUC   Board

Keyboard Mouse   Blackboard   Phone   Speaker

Cat   Printer   Cupboard Cooker   Pen

WORKSHEETS 2

3. Write the names of the parts shown below.

M __ N __ T __ R

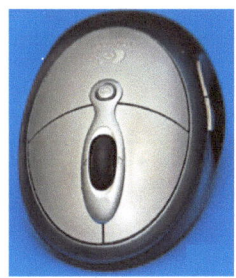

M __ U __ E

K __ Y __ O __ R __

C __ U

WORKSHEETS 2

4. Who am I?

CPU

MONITOR

SPEAKERS

MOUSE

KEYBOARD

a. Use me to point at items shown on the monitor. _____

b. I show photos, games and movies on my screen. _____

c. Use me to write on a computer. _____

d. You need me to listen to songs on the computer. _____

e. I am the brain of the computer. _____

5. Join the wires to the correct place.

WORKSHEETS 2

6. Search for the parts of a computer in the following picture.

7. True or False [Write a T for True or a F for False in each box.]

The CPU is the most important part of a computer. ☐

   a. The Keyboard looks like a television. ☐

   b. The Mouse helps us to point at items. ☐

   c. The Keyboard works like a pencil of the computer. ☐

   a. You can listen to a song on the computer through the speakers. ☐

   d. The Mouse can print what you see on the monitor. ☐

Activity 2

1. Act out being a computer: Play a game where your class acts out being a computer. One student acts as the Keyboard. The teacher uses the keyboard to give the computer a task to do or a problem to solve. Another student acts as the CPU and solves the problem. The CPU tells the answer to the student who is acting as the Monitor, who then shows the answer. Some students can also act as the wires that connect the Keyboard to the CPU and the CPU to the Monitor. You may include a couple of students as Speakers who will sing for the class! You can have your class take turns being different parts of a computer.

2. Draw and colour a computer: Draw a picture of the computer that you are using. Be sure to include all of the computer-related items on the desk in front of you. After your drawing is complete, colour it and write the names of the different parts.

Project
Do project 2 and 3 given in lesson 10.

Explore!

1. Can you see other parts connected to the computer? Find out their names and uses.

2. Just as a computer consists of many parts that have different uses, what are the different parts of a car?

   Find out their names and uses.

Lesson 3

Do's and Don'ts with Computers

In this lesson you will learn the correct way of using computers.

While using computer we should;

1. Be safe – It works on electricity which is dangerous.
2. Handle the computer gently – It is delicate
3. Keep your computer clean – It is sensitive to dust
4. Sit properly on the computer table – You posture is important
5. Share it equally – It is for us all

1. Be safe

Cynthia: There are so many wires coming out of the CPU.

Brian: Yes, there is a wire connected to the electricity socket we should be careful.

Teacher: Very good. A computer works on electricity like your Television so it is important that we be careful.

a) Ask the teacher every time you want to turn the computer on or off. If a wire has come out, ask your teacher to put it back. ✔

b) Do not put your fingers in any opening or slot. ✘

c) Do not pull any wires connected to the CPU. ✘

2. Handle the computer gently

Brian: [Pressing some keys] :These keys are so easy to press.

Teacher: Yes, gentle pressing of each key is enough. A computer is a delicate machine.

      a) Do not bang hard on the Keyboard. ✘

      b) Do not pull parts away from the computer. ✘

3. Keep your computer clean

Brian: I am very hungry. Can we eat now?

Teacher: What if some food falls on the keyboard?

Cynthia: It will become sticky and stop working!

Teacher: Correct.

      a) Keep the computer and its nearby area clean. ✔

      b) Cover the computer when it is not in use. ✔

      c) Do not eat or drink near the computer. ✘

4. Sit properly on the computer table.

Teacher: What will happen if you sit very close to the monitor?

Brian: We will not be able to see the screen clearly. Our eyes will start hurting.

Teacher: Yes, when you are using a computer, your posture is very important.

    a) Keep your chair at the proper height. ✔

    b) Keep a proper distance from the monitor. ✔

    c) Do not keep your hand on the mouse continuously. ✘

5. Share it equally

    a) Take turns for using the Keyboard and the Mouse. ✔

    b) Give space to your classmates while they are using computers. ✔

    c) Do not disturb others by playing loud music. ✘

Brian [To Cynthia]: I have finished playing this game. It is your turn now.

Teacher: It is good that you are taking turns in using the computer. In school, you have to share computers with your friends. Everybody should get an equal chance to learn and play.

Teacher: It is time for you to go home. Tomorrow, we will learn how to use the mouse....

Bye-Bye...

Learning Outcome

After you have studied this lesson, you will be able to:

- Follow safety rules while using computers.
- Be sensitive to the needs of other computer users.
- Follow guidelines for maintenance of the computer.

WORKSHEETS 3

1. See the pictures below.
If it shows the correct way to use a computer, put a tick ✔ mark in the box.
If it shows the wrong way put a cross ✘

a. Mary is cleaning the computer.
   Is this necessary?

b. James and Rebecca are sharing the computer. Is sharing a good habit?

c. Fred is eating near the computer.
   Is this correct?

d. Walter is banging very hard on the Keyboard. Is this the right way to handle the computer?

e. Sarah, Grace and William are pulling out all the wires from their slots. Is it okay for them to do so?

f. The music is being played very loudly. Is this correct?

g. Christine is sitting with a straight back. Fred is bending and is very close to the monitor. Put a tick ✔ mark on the correct position and cross ✘ on the wrong position.

Activity 3

1. **Make a Poster:** Make a poster with the do's and don'ts and put it up in a prominent place in your classroom or computer room.

2. **Share a game with your friends:** Ask your teacher to open the games for you and play them.
   Click Start ==> All Programs ==> Games.

Project

Do project 4 given in lesson 10.

Explore!

1. How will you share the computer to draw a picture?

2. What are the do's and don'ts while watching television?

Lesson 4

How to use a Mouse

In this lesson you will learn
how to use a computer Mouse.

Cynthia: Teacher, you said that we could play music using the computer. Can we do that today?

Teacher: Sure, we use a speaker to listen. Can you tell me how to select the song?

Cynthia: Using the mouse! We already know that a mouse is used to point at items shown on the monitor. When we move the mouse around, the arrow on the screen also moves around.

Teacher: Good. The arrow is called the **mouse pointer**. The mouse is usually kept on a flat surface called the **mouse pad**. Now, how do you play the music?

Brian: I think we should press the buttons on the mouse, but which one?

Teacher: Pressing the button is called a **click**. There are two buttons on the mouse. The button on the left hand side is called the **left button**. The button on the right hand side is called the **right button**. Clicking these buttons tells the computer what to do.

There are three types of mouse clicks:

Left click: Click the left button once. This is used to select an activity after you point to it.

Double click: Click the left button twice, quickly. This is used to start the activity after you have pointed at it.

Right click: Click the right button once. This is used to control the activity after you have started it.

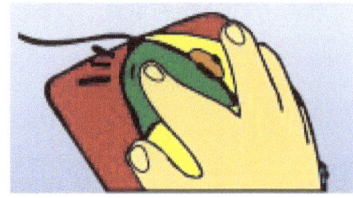  

Brian: To start a song, I have to first point to the song and select it by left click. Then I have to double click for it to play. Am I correct?

Teacher: Very good. You are correct.
Brian now moves the mouse to select the song. While moving, the mouse reaches the end of the mouse pad.

Brian: The mouse pointer is gone. Where is the arrow?

Teacher: When you reach the end of the pad, lift the mouse and place it back in the center.

Brian: Yes. The pointer is back on the screen. Wow! This is fun .What is this wheel like button on the mouse?

Teacher: I will show you.

[Teacher opens a list of names on the screen.]

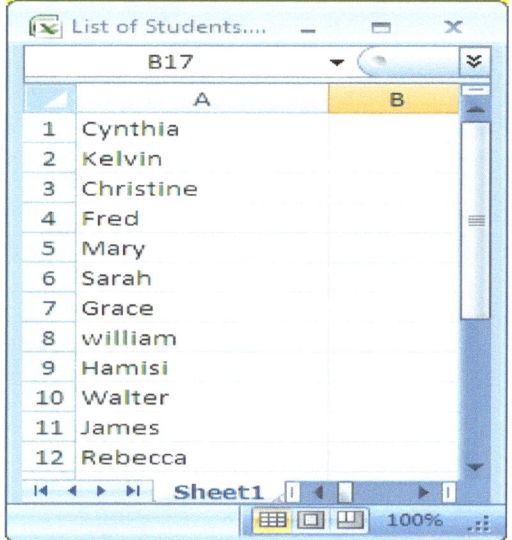

Brian: These are the names of all our friends in the class! Where is my name?

Teacher: Move the wheel and see what happens. Your name will be down below. The wheel between the left and right mouse button is called the **scroll button**. You can move up and down a page using the scroll button.

Cynthia: Can I write my name on the screen?

Teacher: Yes. You can.
Tomorrow I will show you how.
Bye-Bye...

Learning Outcome

After you have studied this lesson, you will be able to:

• Identify the parts of a mouse and their functions.
• Use the mouse buttons for activities.

WORKSHEETS 4

1. What do we use as a pointer when we are reading a book?
   Which is the mouse pointer on the screen?
   Circle both of them

2. In the mouse shown below, colour the left button red, right button green, scroll button blue, and the rest of the mouse yellow.

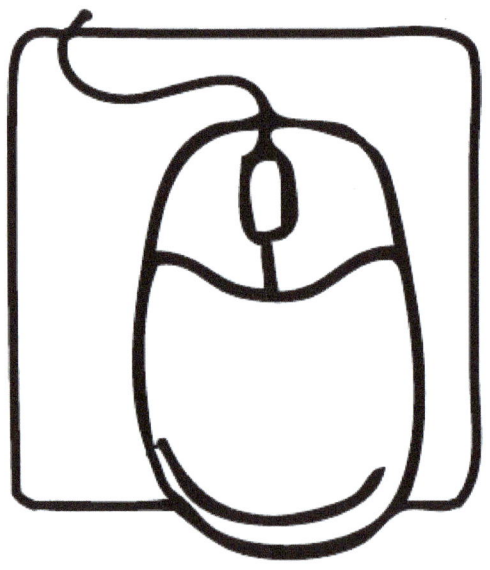

WORKSHEETS 4

3. Circle the words that are related to the Computer Mouse.

Right click   Photo click

Mouse pad   Left click

Rat   Scroll button

Double click   Tail

4. In the mouse shown below, which button will you press for left click? Write 'L' on the left button.
   Which button will you press for right click? Write 'R' on the right button.

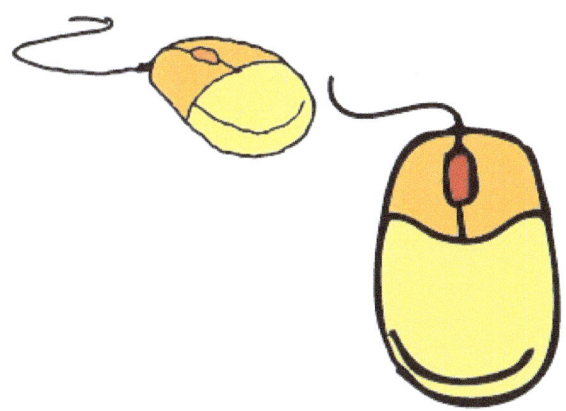

5. Match the columns.

Left click   Move up and down a page

Right click   Start an activity

Scroll button   Select an activity

Double click   Control the activity

Activity 4

1. Play games that require the use of a mouse: Ask the teacher to help you find them.

Project

Do project 5 given in lesson 10.

Explore!

1. Click on various items on the screen and see if the mouse pointer changes. When does this happen?

2. Look at the computer mouse in your school and in other places. Do they all look the same?

Lesson 5

How to use a Keyboard

 In this lesson you will learn how to use a Keyboard.

Teacher: Today we will play some games. First tell me, what do you use to write in your book?

Cynthia: We use a pencil or a pen. Our teacher uses a chalk to write on the board.

Brian: I have seen my sister use a keyboard to write on the computer.

Teacher: The Keyboard is an important part of a computer. What do you see on it?

Brian: It has many small buttons. Some of them have alphabets and numbers written on them. There are also some words like 'Enter' written on them.

Cynthia: The keyboard is connected by a wire to the CPU of the computer.

Teacher: Right. We can use a keyboard to give instructions to the computer. The buttons on the keyboard are called **keys**.

Alphabet Keys

The keys on which you see alphabets: A – Z are called **alphabet keys**. These are used to write words.

Number Keys

The keys on which you see numbers: 0 - 9 are called number keys. These are used to write numbers.

Special Keys

The keys on which you see words are called special keys. These are used for specific tasks such as moving to the next line on a page.

Teacher opens a Text Editor.

Teacher: Try to type your names using the keyboard. Can you find the alphabets in your name on the keyboard?

Brian: [types his name] Yes. My name now appears on the monitor! Whatever I typed on the keyboard is now shown on the monitor.

Teacher: Remember, your posture while using a keyboard is important. Sit straight while typing. Press softly on the keys.

Brian: [continues typing "briancynthia"]: How do I leave a space between the names?

Teacher: Use the **Space bar**.

Space bar

While you are typing, you can press the Space bar to create spaces.
This is usually the longest key on the last row of the keyboard. It may not have anything written on it.

Brian: I made a mistake while typing. How do I erase it?

Teacher: Use the **Backspace** key.

Backspace

While you are typing, you can press the Backspace key to erase letters. It is usually the last key in the row of numbers. This may look different on different keyboards.

Brian [after a lot of typing]: How do I go to the next line?

Teacher: Use the **Enter** key. Press this key once to go to the next line.

Enter Key

While you are typing, the Enter key is used to move to the next line.
It is usually found at the end of the middle row of alphabets. The
Enter key is also used for other actions which we will learn later.

Teacher: Now you can play the game that you played after lesson 2, Activity
2, 1.

The children play the game for some time and soon it was time for
them to go home.

Brian: This was fun. Tomorrow, can you show us how to paint using a
computer?

Teacher:. Yes. Tomorrow we can explore how to draw, paint and much more.
Bye-Bye...

Learning Outcome
After you have studied this lesson,
you will be able to:

- Use a keyboard for entering words
  and numbers.
- Use the special keys to enter text.

WORKSHEETS 5

1. Identify the ENTER key and colour them in Red.
   Colour all the ALPHABET keys in Green.

2. Colour the alphabets in the word COMPUTERS.

3. Tick the correct way to sit while using the keyboard.

Activity 5

1. Play games that require the use of a keyboard.
   Ask your teacher on how to open them.

2. Enter the following words on the computer. Ask your teacher on how to open the text editor Notepad)

   a. Mouse

   b. Keyboard

   c. Monitor

   d. space bar

Project
Do project 6 given in lesson 10.

Explore!
1. How will you write the number 2015 using the keyboard?

2. How will you write your name in CAPITAL and small letters?

Lesson 6

How to paint using a Computer

In this lesson you will learn how to perform simple computer activities using Paint.

Brian: Teacher, we want to draw and paint today. Do we double click on one of these small pictures on the screen?

Teacher: Yes, these small pictures on the screen are called **icons**.
Double click on the **Paint** icon.

Cynthia double clicks on the paint icon, points to the empty space that opens up on the screen and asks.

Cynthia: Do we draw and paint here? Do we also use our crayons on the monitor?

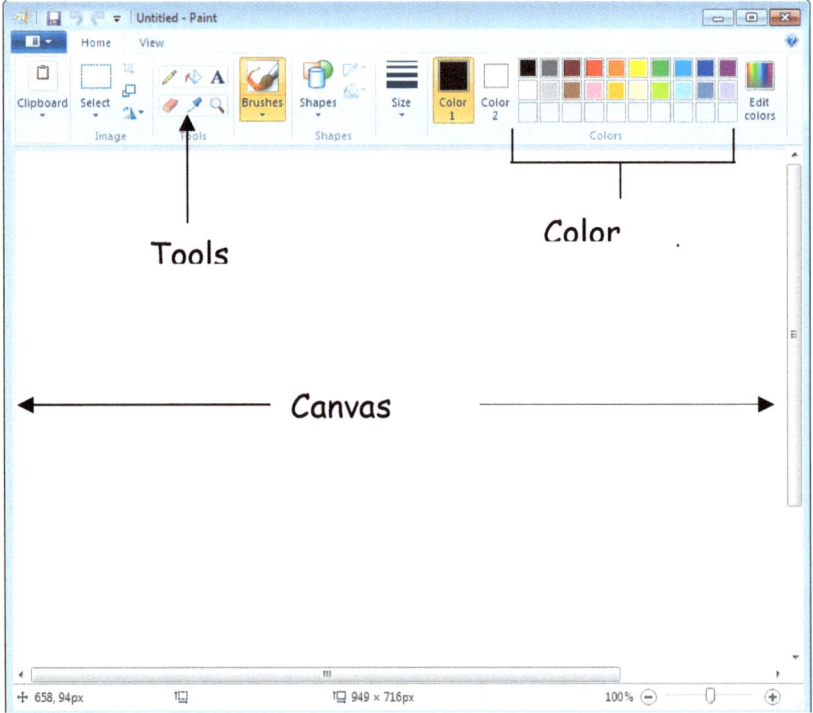

Teacher: We use the blank space in the window. It is like a page in your drawing book where you can draw and paint. This is called the **canvas area**. We do not use our crayons to draw here.

Brian : I see 'Tools' written on the screen. What does it mean?

Teacher : When you draw on a paper, you use pencil, brushes, colors and eraser. These are your drawing tools. In the same way, the tools for drawing using a computer can be found under **Tools**. A set of tools is called a **Toolbar**. The various choices in any toolbar are called the **Options**.

Teacher: Click on any of the **Shapes** to open a shape. Choose the area to draw the shape. Draw it by pressing and dragging the left mouse button. Color your shape by picking up either the color picker or color filler from the **Tools** section first the select the desired color from the **color pallet**. Finish by pressing the left mouse button at the area you want to color.

Cynthia: I want to draw my own picture and then color it.
What should I click on to do this?

Teacher: You can do this by selecting the **New** option under Tools. You can then use the Paint option in the Toolbar to start drawing.

Cynthia: I want to draw a 'flower' in red color. Should I click on the **Colors** Toolbar?

Color Palette

Teacher: Correct. The Colors Toolbar is called the **Color Palette**. Select 'red' color and the 'brush' tool with which you want to draw. Then draw on the canvas area. Colors in the color palette can be used with many of the tools. For example, select a 'yellow' color and then select the 'fill' tool. Now, click inside the Sun you have drawn, to fill it with yellow color.

Teacher: All the Shape items such as square and circle are grouped together in the **Shapes** toolbar.

Brian: Oh, this is just like all the writing items such as pencil, sharpener and eraser are grouped together in the pencil box.

Cynthia: All the food items such as rice and beans are grouped together in my lunch box.

Teacher: Very good examples. Now look at the different shapes in the toolbar.

Cynthia [Pointing to Pentagon]: A Pentagon has five sides. I know that.

Teacher: Everything around you has a shape. Can you draw and paint some objects using the tools?

Cynthia and Brian use drawing and painting tools and complete the following two picture.

Cynthia: I want to draw and paint one more picture. I do not want to erase this picture.

Teacher: Ok. Use the **Save** option to save the picture that you have drawn. The computer saves the picture in a file. You will learn more about files later.

Teacher: It is time to go home. Tomorrow you can do more painting. Bye-Bye...

Learning Outcome
After you have studied this lesson,
you will be able to:

- Identify icons associated with its activity.
- Draw and color paintings in Paint.
- Use options in toolbar of an activity.

WORKSHEETS 6

1. Match the following buttons to their functions:

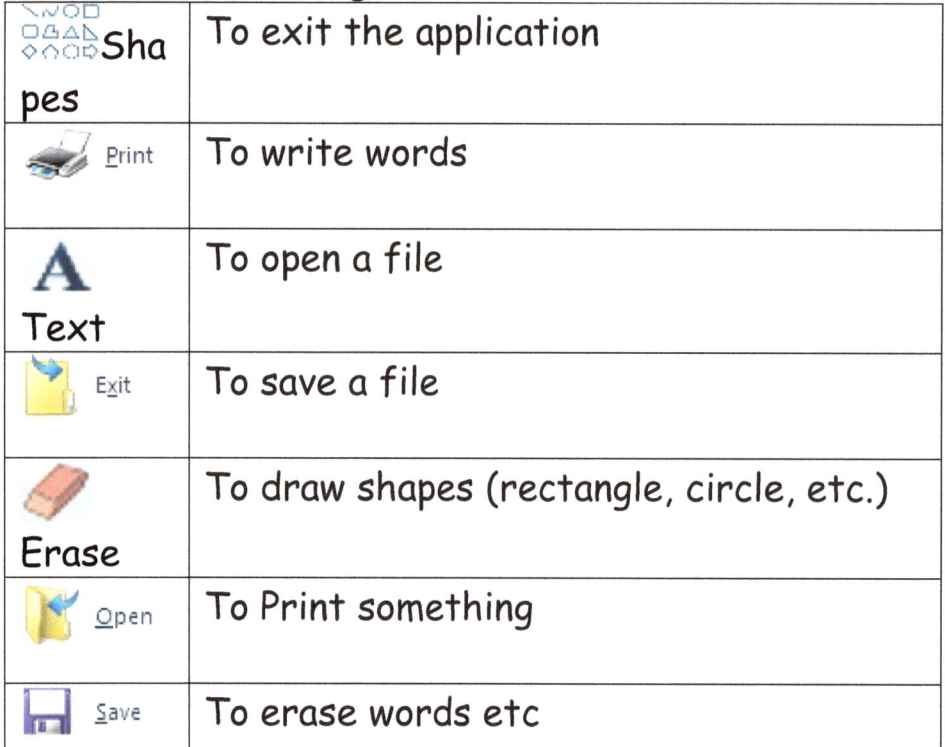

Shapes	To exit the application
Print	To write words
A Text	To open a file
Exit	To save a file
Erase	To draw shapes (rectangle, circle, etc.)
Open	To Print something
Save	To erase words etc

2.

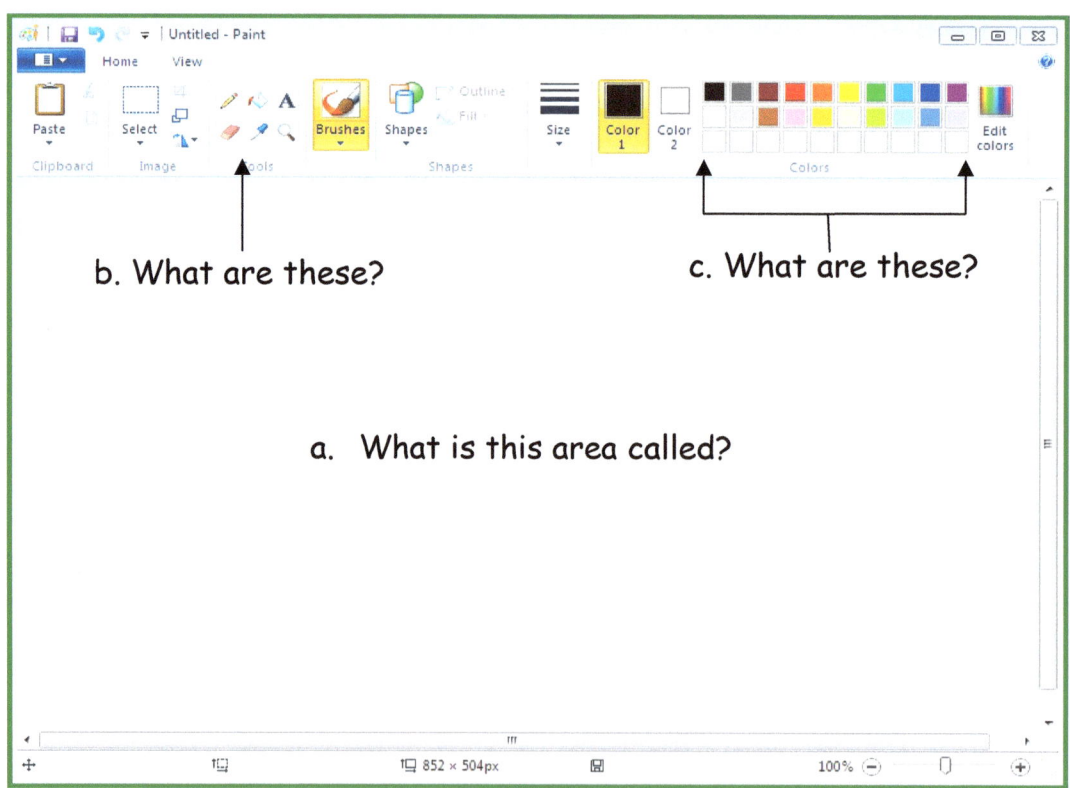

b. What are these?

c. What are these?

a. What is this area called?

Activity 6

1. Draw the following picture using the Paint application.

2. Open Paint and create your own drawings. Start the activity by clicking on its icon and open a new painting and draw them for colouring. Explore the colour tools and colour the drawings. Save the file after you complete the task.

Project
Do project 7 given in lesson 10.

Explore!

1. Where can you find the different colours and shapes in Paint?

2. Search for △ in the shapes, draw it and color it with blue color.

Lesson 7

More Actions using Paint

In this lesson you will learn more actions common to many activities, through Paint.

Cynthia: Hello Teacher, I want to draw a new picture today. Should I click the **New** option to get a blank canvas?

Teacher: Yes. You can use the New option to get a blank canvas. You can draw and paint your new picture here.

Cynthia: [after drawing the picture]: You said that, we should use the **Save** option to save the picture in a file. What is a file?

Teacher: A **File** is like a page in your notebook. Every time you use a new canvas, the picture will be saved as a new file.

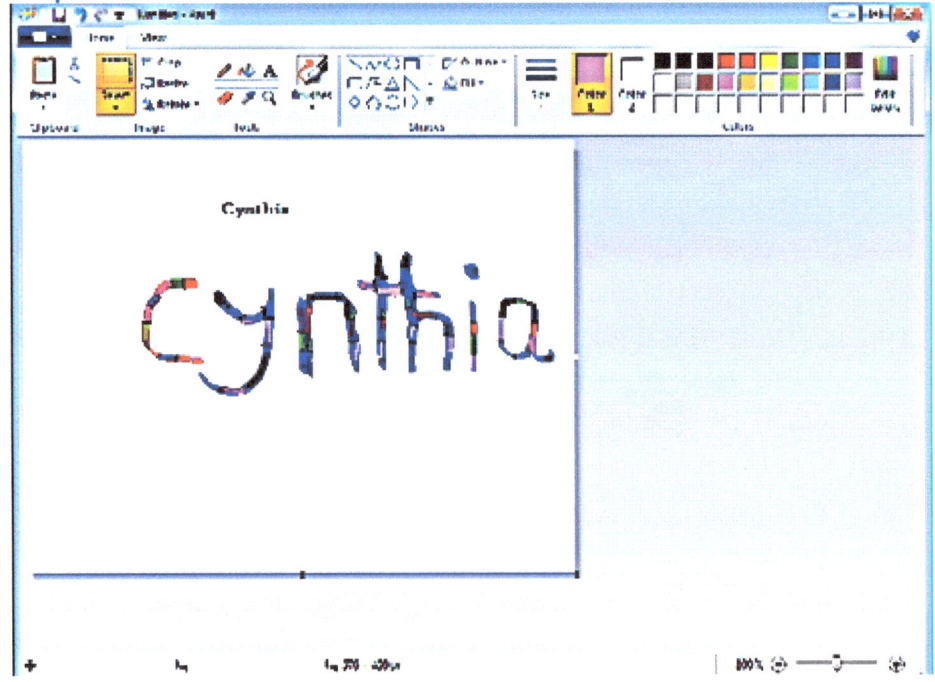

Brian: I clicked the Open option. It shows many saved pictures. There is also the picture that I drew last time!

Teacher: The **Open** option gives a list of all the saved files. You can continue to draw and change any of these pictures.

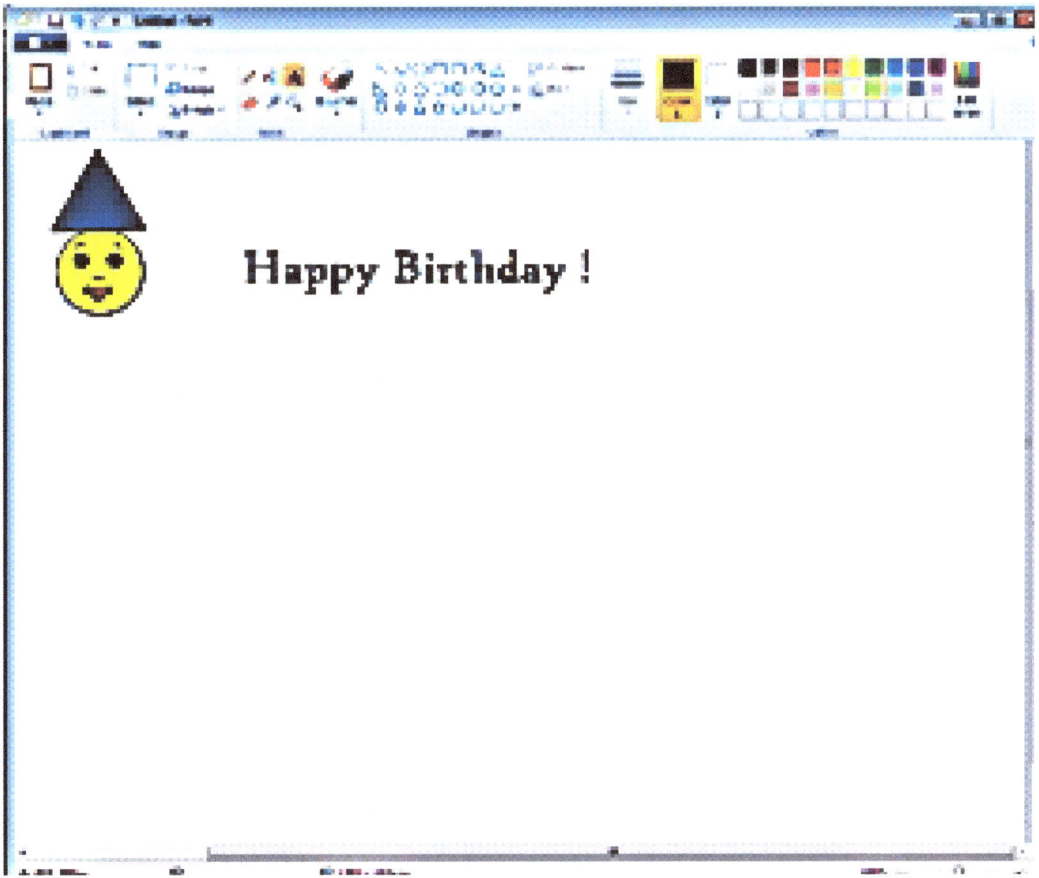

Brian selects the picture that he likes and adds the line "Happy Birthday' to it. He uses the **Print** option from the toolbar to print the birthday card.

Brian: Now when I try to save this changed picture, will I lose the old one?

Teacher: Click on **Save** and see what happens.

Brian clicks on the Paint icon and sees this screen:

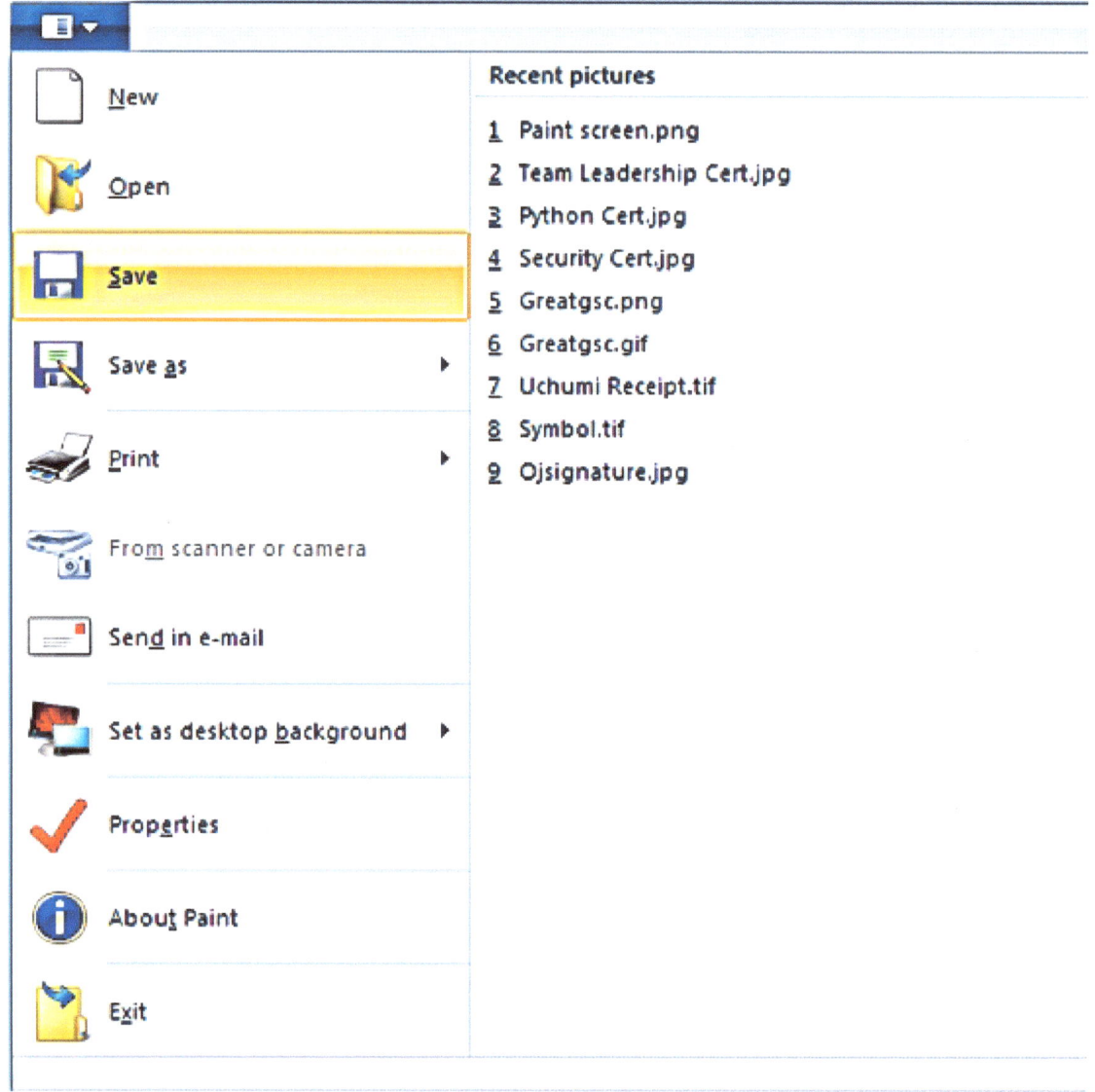

Then Brian clicks on Save and the following screen is seen:

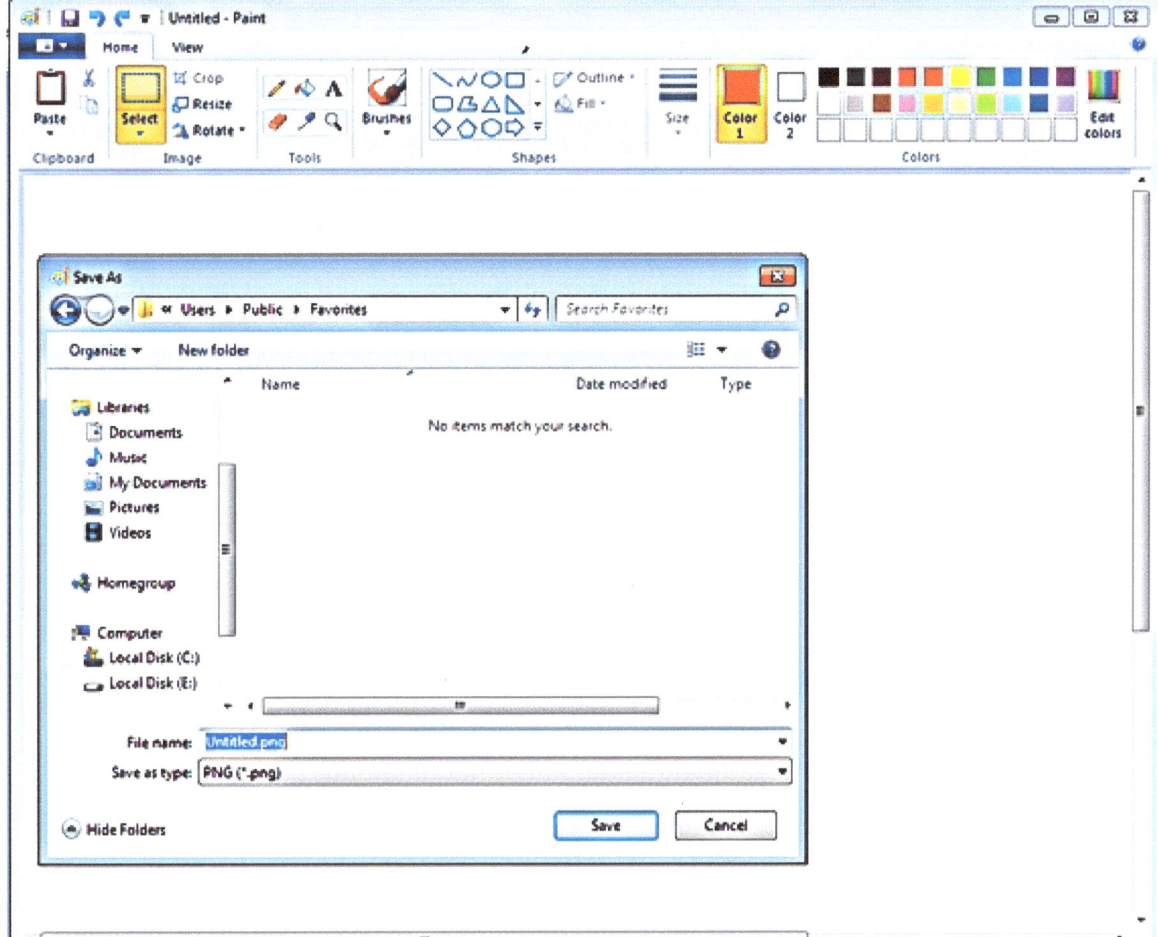

Teacher: This is called a **Dialog box**. See here, it asks how you want to save the picture. Type in the name of the picture you want save, where it is written 'File name. Then you can choose 'Save' or 'Cancel' accordingly.

Teacher: Remember to always close the activities once you finish working on a computer.

Cynthia: I clicked on **Exit** to close the activity. What is this new dialog box?

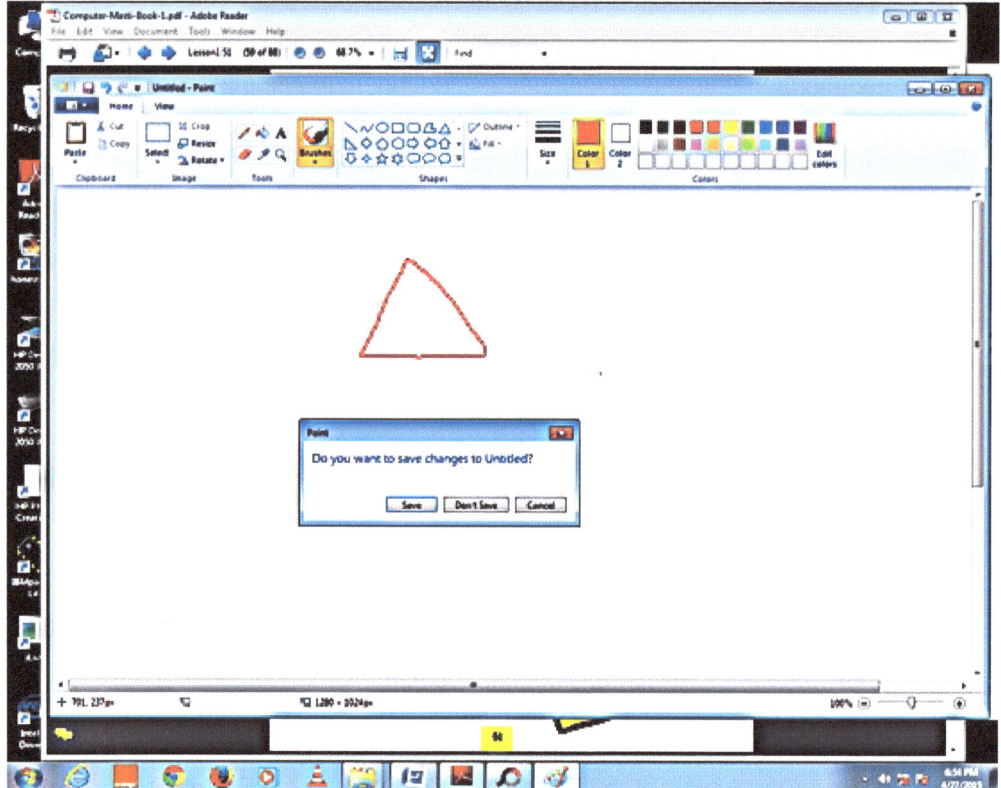

Teacher: You did not **Save** your picture before you clicked **Exit**. So the computer gives you a chance to save the picture. If you were just exploring the options and don't want to save the picture, you can choose Don't Save and exit without saving the picture.

I Shall I tell you one more interesting fact? The actions that you have learnt today - **New, Open, Save,** and **Exit** – are the same in all the other activities also! You have to just look for them.

Bye-Bye...

Learning Outcome

After you have studied this lesson, you will be able to:

- Describe what is a file.
- Open a new or existing.
- Save and Print a file.

WORKSHEETS 7

1. Match the following buttons to their functions:

A	B
Print	To write words
Save	Exit Application
A Text	To open a file
Exit	To save a file
Erase	To Print something
Open	To erase something

2. Open a picture in paint and color it.

Activity 7

1. Start the Paint application and open a new page. Draw a tall tree, a short plant and grass. Use the different tool options, such as Paint, and Lines. Save the file and quit the activity.

2. Make a greeting card for your friend using the different tool options. Save the file and quit the activity.

3. Click on Open and check all the pictures you have drawn.

Explore!

1. What are the different kinds of brushes that can be used to draw a line? Find out how you can draw a line of stars, dots and squires.

2. After you draw a picture, search for the Mirror option and use it.

Lesson 8

How to Play Music on a Computer

In this lesson you will learn how to use a Windows Media Player.

Cynthia: Let us listen to music using the computer.

Brian double clicks on the music file icon on the computer. Both of them are listening to the music as the Teacher appears.

Brian: I have seen the same buttons at home on my CD player !

Cynthia: Me too, I have also seen them on a Cassette player.

Teacher: Very good music! Do you enjoy listening to music? Today let us learn how to use the Windows media player on a computer. Take a look at these buttons. [Points to the control buttons]

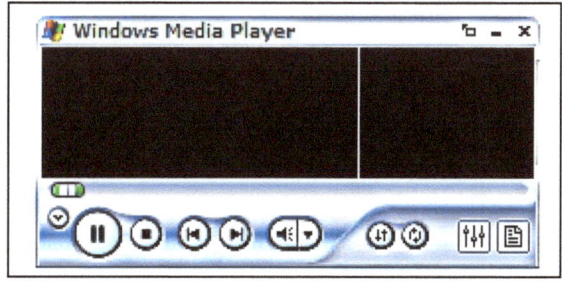

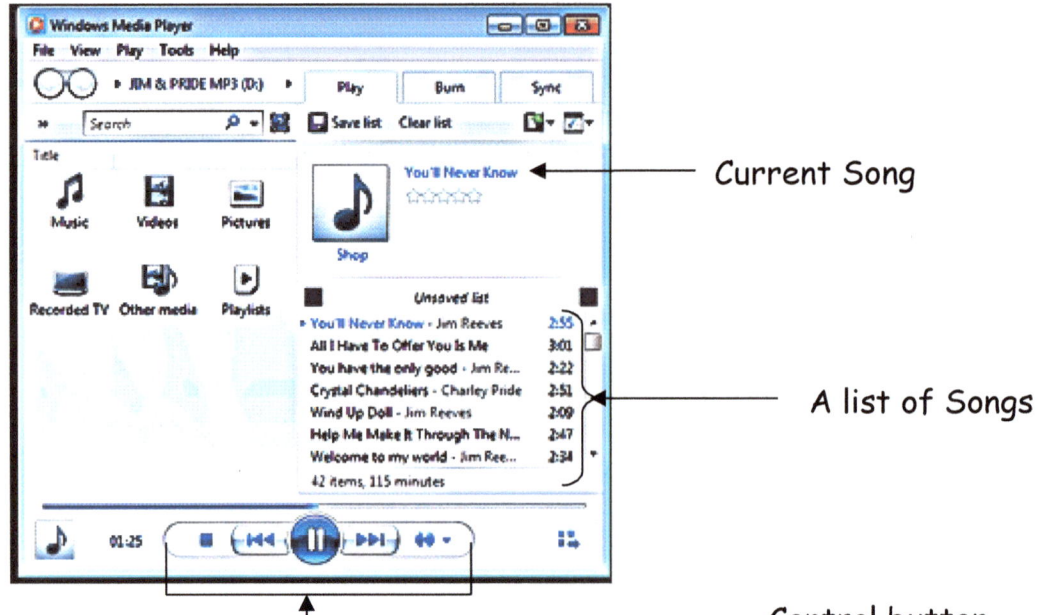

Current Song

A list of Songs

Control button

Teacher: A CD player plays songs that are stored on the CD. A cassette player plays songs that are stored on the cassette. The songs are stored as music files on the computer. Music can also be stored on a DVD, a Flash disk or Memory card.

Cynthia [pointing to the music file icon]:
This is similar to Paint files. There is one file for each song.

Music icon

Teacher: Very good. Now you know that we should not disturb others by playing loud music. Can you please reduce the volume?

Cynthia: [clicks on some button] Oh! The song has stopped.

Teacher: The song stopped as you clicked the **Pause** button. If you move the mouse pointer over the buttons, it will show the name of the button. Now start the song again.

Cynthia [clicks the Play button]: The music is playing from where it stopped!

Brian: The play button once it clicked it changes into Pause why?

Teacher: The Windows media player knows that when the song is playing you can pause it. When it is not playing it automatically changes and waits for you to press Play.

Teacher: Yes. When you Pause a song and then press **Play**, it will continue playing from where it had stopped. Now find the Volume button.

Cynthia clicks the **Volume** button and tries to reduce the sound. But nothing happens. Brian also tries but is not able to reduce the sound.

Teacher: Do you see a slider that comes up when you click the Volume button?

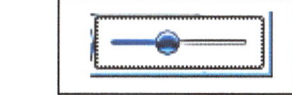

You can increase or decrease the volume by moving this slider.
To move the slider, first point the mouse on it.

Then keep the left button of the mouse pressed and drag it.
The trick is to keep the mouse button pressed while dragging.

Brian [dragging the slider Left and Right]: Hey, this is fun! Can we play a different song now?

Teacher: Do you remember what you did in Paint to open a picture? I told you that you will find the same actions in other activities too!

Brian: Yes! I can use the **Open** option.

He searches the toolbar of the music player till he finds the **Open** option. Brian and Cynthia explore the controls and listen to more music.

Teacher: You may have different music players on your computer, but they will have similar buttons.

➢ Play starts the song.
➢ Stop stops the song completely.
➢ Pause stops the song. Pressing Pause or Play again will continue the song from where it had stopped.
➢ Rewind and Forward to jump to a different part of the song or a different song.
➢ Slider can be used to increase or decrease the volume.
➢ Mute turns off the volume when it is pressed. The song continues to play, but you cannot hear it. Pressing Mute again will turn the volume back on.

Cynthia: Teacher, I see a very small music player window at the bottom of the screen. When I click on it, the big music player window disappears. When I click on it again, the big window is back again. What is happening?

Teacher: The bar at the bottom of the screen is called the **Taskbar**. When you open any activity, a small window of that activity appears on the Taskbar. Tomorrow you can learn more about the Taskbar and windows. Bye-Bye...

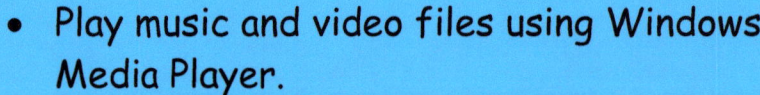

Learning Outcome
After you have studied this lesson, you will be able to:

- Play music and video files using Windows Media Player.
- Use play, pause. Stop, volume control buttons on player.

WORKSHEETS 8

1. Match the following:

2. Match the Microsoft Media Player button with its use:

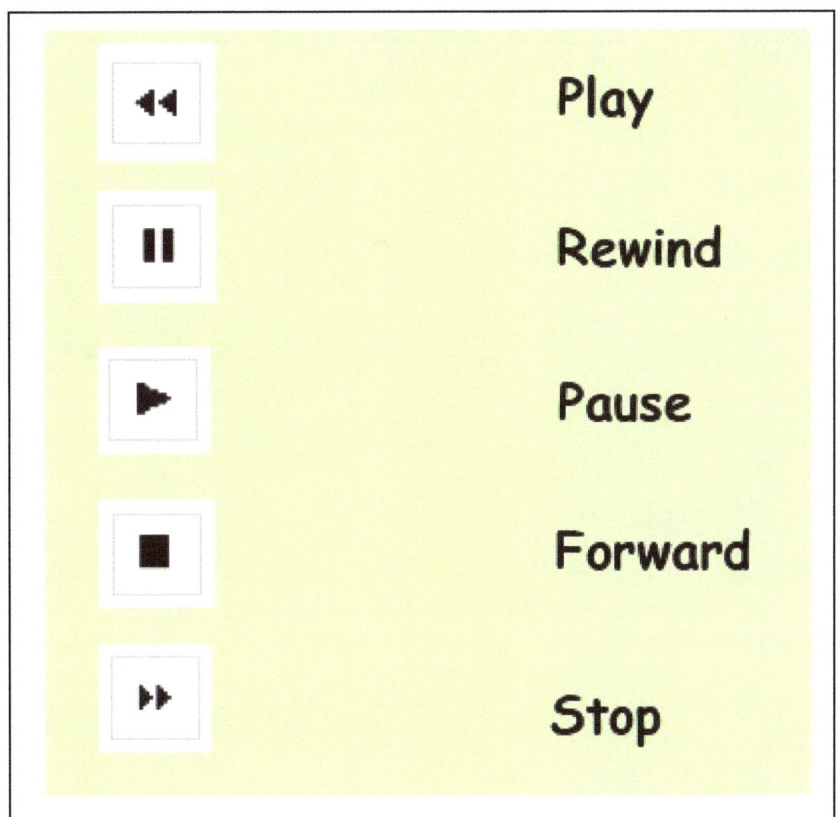

Activity 8

1. Open Games by going through Start --->All programs ---> Games

   Open and Play the Purble Place

2. Open Games by going through Start --->All programs ---> Games

   Open and play Purble Shop

3. Open Games by going through Start --->All programs ---> Games

   Open and play Purble Pairs

Explore!
1. Find a music or Video CD and play it on the computer using a media player.

2. How is a music file different from a video file?

Lesson 9

Exploring the Desktop

In this lesson you will learn about the computer Desktop.

Cynthia and Brian were exploring the computer as the teacher walks in.

Teacher: Hello children. So you are exploring the activities on the Desktop?

Cynthia: Yes. Why is this screen called the Desktop?

Teacher: How do you arrange all your books on a desk? If all the books are neatly arranged, is it not easy to find them? In the same way, the screen where all the icons are arranged is called a Desktop. Icons of activities that we use often are kept on the **Desktop**. The bar at the bottom of the screen is called the **Taskbar**.

Cynthia double clicks on music icon and then the paint icon.

Cynthia: Two windows have opened. So, can I play music and also paint?

Teacher: Yes. You can. You can start more than one activity on the computer. Each time you double click an icon, it opens a new **Window** for that activity.

Brian: Clicking on a window brings it to the front.

Teacher: Correct. Whenever you click on a Window, the computer brings it in front and allows you to use that activity.

The top bar of a window is called the **Title bar**. You can recognize the activity in a window by the title on the title bar.

Brian: [Clicks the 🔲 button on the title bar of the Paint window]: The paint window has gone! How can I get it back?

After Minimising

Teacher: You clicked the **Minimise** button. This button is at the top right corner and makes any window very small. See here on the Taskbar.

The Paint activity window has become a small button. Clicking this Paint button on the Taskbar will open the Paint window again.

The taskbar has one button for each window on the Desktop. So, all the activities that have been started can be seen in the **taskbar**.

Brian is watching the windows when Cynthia clicks on the Paint window.

Cynthia [clicks the button on the music window]: The music window has gone! The music has also stopped. I clicked on at the top right corner of the window.

Teacher: Ah! You clicked the **Close** button. This at the top right corner of the window is used to close the activity. See here, it has gone from the taskbar also.

Cynthia: The picture on Brian's desktop is different from mine. Can we change these pictures?

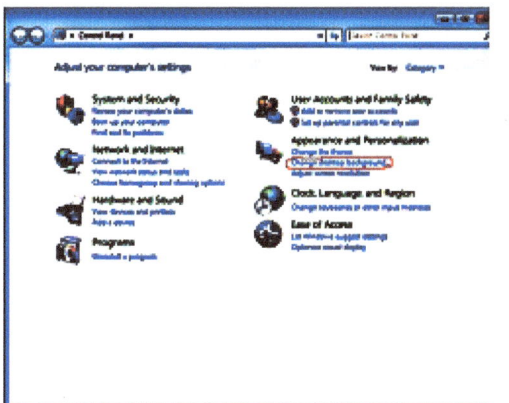

Teacher: Yes. You can. You can make the desktop look any way you like. The picture on the desktop is called the **Wallpaper** or **Desktop Background**.

Click on the round windows logo on the bottom left corner of your screen. A dialog box will open.

On the right hand side of the dialog box, click on the **Control Panel**, then you will see this screen on the left.

Click on the option to **change desktop background**. The following screen will come up.

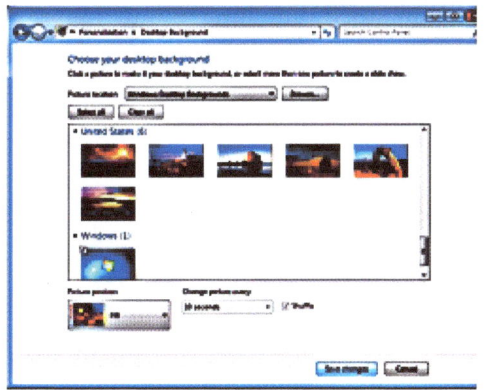

Using the scroll bar on the side, pick another picture you wish to use by clicking on it.

Finish change by clicking on the **Save changes** button. Yes! Indeed, your desktop background has changed.

Cynthia: That means we can also use our own paintings as wallpaper.

Teacher: Yes. You can add more wallpapers to the ones that are already there. Explore all the options in the dialog box at your home.
Bye- Bye...

Learning Outcome

After you have studied this lesson, you will be able to:

- Identify the elements of a Desktop and window.
- Run multiple activities from Desktop and switch between them.
- Change Wallpaper of a desktop.

WORKSHEETS 9

1. Observe the following picture and answer the questions:

Mark the following.
   a. Wallpaper
   b. Taskbar
   c. Icons

2. Fill in the blanks

   a. W __ L __ P __ __ E __

   b. D E __ K T __ P

   c. T __ S __ B __ R

   d. S C __ E_ N

WORKSHEETS 9

3. Match the columns:

R P A E P L W A L	DESKTOP
H S F I N I	WALLPAPER
E D K S O T P	TASKBAR
R B A S A T K	FINISH

4. Rebecca wants to change the wallpaper of her desktop. Help her find the steps she should follow by numbering the steps starting from the first step taking number 1 and the last one taking number 9.

☐ Left click the mouse on round Windows logo on the bottom left corner of your screen.

☐ Click on the 'Change Desktop Background' option.

☐ The dialog box opens with several pictures

☐ Use the Scrollbar to select the Desktop Background of your choice.

☐ Another Dialog box opens.

☐ Click on the 'Control Panel'

☐ Click on 'Safe changes button' to finish

☐ A dialog box opens

☐ Wallpaper changes

Activity 9

1. Draw a picture of an flower. While drawing, listen to music.
2. Change the desktop using a variety of pictures and styles as follows:

      b. Picture centered on desktop

      a. Picture Stretched on Desktop

      c. Picture Fits on Desktop

Explore!
1. What else do you see on the taskbar of the desktop? Time? Date? Click and find out about these.
2. In addition to double click, are there other ways to start an activity?
3. What happens if you press the square button on the top right corner of a window? Does the window change?

Lesson 10
Projects

Project 1 (Lesson 1)

a. While you go out with your family, make a note of all the places where computers are used. What are they used for? How was work done without computers? Narrate what you learnt in the class. The teacher moderates the discussion in the class.

b. People from different occupations use computers for different purposes. Find who uses computers and for what. For example, a doctor uses it to keep records of his patients. Each student can choose a different profession, gather information and talk about it in the class.

Project 2 (Lesson 2)

Collect pictures of different kinds of computers and computer parts. Paste them together on a sheet and put it up in the class.

Project 3 (Lesson 2)

a. Use Manila Papers, scissors, glue/tape, and crayons to make your own computer parts. Divide the class into groups of five students. Each group makes one of the following parts: keyboard, monitor, CPU, mouse and speakers. Ask your teacher to provide you with materials that are easily available to make wires! Put them all together with the help of the teacher.

b. Make puppets of computer parts by sticking the parts you made. Lift them up with your hand and tell the class what the computer part does!

c. List out things that have wires. Find out why wires are not seen in some of parts.

Project 4 (Lesson 3)

a. Learn the correct posture for sitting while you are reading and writing. Find out why they are the correct ways and share it with your classmates.

b. What are the games that require you to stand or sit in a particular posture? Play two such games in your school playground.

c. Just like computers, what are the other things in your house that you have to keep clean and use safely? Find out why you should be careful in using those things and discuss in the class.

Project 5 (Lesson 4)

a. List the things that have a wheel like object that can move/rotate something as the scroll button of the mouse does? Find out if they are of different sizes and what they are used for. Talk about what you learnt in the class.

b. Find out the importance of a wheel in machines. Share what you learnt about it with your classmates.

Project 6 (Lesson 5)

List all the instruments that have keys to be pressed to use them (e.g. piano, type writer). Collect pictures of the listed instruments and paste them in your scrapbook. Find out how they are the same or different from the keyboard of a computer and discuss in class.

Project 7 (Lessons 7)

Draw different shapes using the Paint activity on the computer.

www.ingramcontent.com/pod-product-compliance
Lightning Source LLC
Chambersburg PA
CBHW050743180526
45159CB00003B/1330